How to Plan a
Hawaiian Luau

Dawn Mahealani Douglas

HOW TO PLAN A HAWAIIAN LUAU

HOW TO PLAN A HAWAIIAN LUAU

CONTENTS

History of Luau 1

Hosting a Luau 3

Purpose 4

Place 5

Food 6

Drinks 8

Decorations 10

Dress 12

Music 13

Entertainment 14

Hawaiian Words 17

Meaning of Aloha 18

HOW TO PLAN A HAWAIIAN LUAU

HOW TO PLAN A HAWAIIAN LUAU

HISTORY OF LUAU

The luau was an ancient ritual and social gathering celebrating a special achievement, war victory, canoe launch, or Hawaiian god. Originally referred toas an ʻaha ʻaina: ʻaha meaning 'gathering' and ʻaina meaning 'meal,' the gathering did not include women or the lower class as they were forbidden to dine with men or consume certain foods. In 1819, King Kamehameha II invited women for the first time and the gathering became known as a luau, named after a dish, made of kalo (taro) leaves and chicken baked in coconut milk. Attendees sat on lauhala mats and ate with their hands while centerpieces consisted of flowers, ferns, and palm leaves. Blowing the pu (conch shell) signified the beginning of the ceremony.

Luaus of the past were also held to celebrate a child's first birthday or baby luau, other birthdays, graduations, and weddings. Leis were given to guests as a symbol of love or honor. Some luaus may have included Hawaiian hula, the native dance form, and Samoan fire knife along with traditional foods like kalua pig prepared in an imu (underground oven), poi made from taro, lomi lomi salmon, and haupia. Hawaii's rapid growth of tourism in the 1950s transformed the luau to a tourist attraction where visitors could experience the tradition of the luau of the past. Visitors could enjoy traditional food, and entertainment began to include music and dance from a few Polynesian islands like Hawaii, Tahiti, Samoa, and Aotearoa (New Zealand).

Hale O Lono (House of Lono)

HOSTING A LUAU

The luau has expanded to Mainland USA as a popular party theme. Yes, it is acceptable for anyone to host a luau so long as it is respectful of Hawaiian culture and tradition. Cultural practitioners who cater to a "tourist" clientele here on the mainland, are often asked what is respectful and what is not respectful as well as specifics to make their luaus more authentic. The purpose of this guide is to help answer those questions. Enjoy with my aloha!

Backyard Luau

PURPOSE

Some purposes of traditional luaus are discussed in the history section,
but today, luaus are held for any celebratory occasion. Remember that a luau is not
strictly a summer event, but also happens year-round in Hawaii and on the mainland.
Below are a few examples.

Birthdays
Baby showers
Weddings
Anniversaries
Graduations
Retirement parties
Holidays
Seasons
Grand openings
Award banquets
Fundraisers
Festivals

PLACE

Depending on convenience and weather, a luau can be held indoors or outdoors. Consider your own home or backyard or place of business to keep cost down. If you want to book a venue, event halls, public parks, hotels, and restaurants are options. Be sure to check how many guests the venue will hold, what type of décor and entertainment is permitted, and if liability insurance is required. Always have a back-up plan so the event can go on even if it rains (i.e., cover or indoor area for guests and entertainers).

FOOD

Kalua pig is the traditional main dish at a luau and if you want to try your hand at preparing it, you will find a recipe here modified without the use of the imu. Chicken and fish are alternatives for a main dish. Favorite side items include poi, lomi lomi salmon, and chicken long rice. It is important to note that the kalo or taro plant is revered in Hawaiian culture, considered the brother of man, and parts of the taro plant are used in cooking including the leaves wrapped around food as it is cooked and served on the plate. Poi is made from the corm mashed with water and allowed to ferment. While you may not have access to taro leaves in your area, you may be able to find poi. Haupia is a coconut pudding popular throughout all of Polynesia.

Kumu Kea's Oven-Roasted Kalua Pig

4 pounds pork butt
4 tablespoons liquid smoke
2 tablespoons Hawaiian salt or other coarse ground salt
Score the pork butt by making cuts ¼ inch deep and 1 inch apart. Rub the pork with the salt and liquid smoke. If you are lucky enough to have ti leaves, de-bone them and fasten them around the pork butt. Wrap the pork bundle in aluminum foil and allow to stand at room temperature for about 30 minutes. Preheat oven to 500 degrees. Place the pork on a meat rack above a shallow roasting pan. Bake for 45 minutes, then reduce to 400 degrees and cook for 3 ½ hours more. When done, cool slightly and then shred the pork. Taste and add more liquid smoke or salt if needed. Serves 10.

Lomi Lomi Salmon

2 cups salted salmon, diced
6 tomatoes, diced
2 small red onions, diced
½ cup green onion, thinly sliced
1 Hawaiian chili pepper or 1/8 teaspoon red pepper flakes
Combine all ingredients and mix well. Serve well chilled. Serves 12.

6

Chicken Long Rice

4 ounces long rice
20 dried shiitake mushrooms
4 cups chicken broth
2 pounds skinless, boneless chicken, cubed
2-inch finger of fresh ginger, crushed
1 medium onion, minced
2 cups thinly sliced celery
2 carrots, julienned
6 green onions, cut in 1-inch lengths

Soak long rice in warm water for 1 hour. Soak mushrooms in warm water for 20 minutes. Drain. Remove stems and slice caps. Pour chicken broth into a large pot, add chicken and ginger, and simmer for 5 minutes. Add onion, celery, carrots, and mushrooms, and simmer another 4 to 5 minutes. Drain long rice and cut into 3-inch lengths. Add long rice and green onions to the pot and stir. Cook an additional 5 minutes or until long rice becomes translucent. Serves 12.

Haupia

6 cups canned or fresh coconut milk
1 cup cornstarch
1 cup sugar
½ teaspoon salt
1 cup crushed pineapple

Drain pineapple, squeeze out excess liquid, and set aside. Combine coconut milk, cornstarch, sugar, and salt. Stir until cornstarch is dissolved. Cook on medium heat stirring constantly until it reaches the boiling point, and then reduce to low. When it begins to thicken, add the pineapple, and mix well. Pour into individual dessert bowls or sorbet glasses and serve either warm or cold topped with whipped cream. To serve cold, chill for at least 1 hour. Serves 12.

Other Options

It is perfectly acceptable to keep it simple with food you can find in your area. Poke dishes are popular as well as chicken wings. Macaroni salad, sweet potatoes, breadfruit, and fresh fruit are all great sides, and macadamia nut cookies can make a simple dessert item.

DRINKS

When someone says luau, tropical drinks most likely come to mind. The Mai Tai, said to be "out of this world" by his friend from Tahiti, was created by Trader Vic Bergeron in 1944 and made its debut at The Royal Hawaiian Hotel in 1953. The Blue Hawaii was created by Harry Yee, a bartender at the Hilton Hawaiian Village around 1957 for the Bols company.

Mai Tai

1-ounce light rum
1-ounce dark rum
½ ounce orange curacao
½ ounce orgeat syrup
2 ounces pineapple juice
1 ounce orange juice
Squeeze of lime juice
Mix in a shaker with ice. Garnish with lime shell and sprig of fresh mint.

Blue Hawaii

2 tablespoons blue curacao
2 tablespoons vodka
1 tablespoon fresh lime juice
2 teaspoons sugar syrup
4 tablespoons pineapple juice
Mix in a shaker. Garnish with pineapple wedge.

Non-Alcoholic Drink or Kids' Drink: Banana Mango Smoothie

3-5 fresh bananas
2 fresh mangoes

Squeeze of honey
¼ cup fresh coconut milk or apple juice
Serve blended.

DECORATIONS

Luau decorations do not have to break the bank. Take your cues from the luaus of the past and use flowers (hibiscus), leaves (palms), fruits (pineapples), and shells as the focal points on tables and throughout the event space. Tiki torches are great for mood lighting. Adding a lei greeting for your guests is a special touch steeped in Hawaiian tradition and meaning. Giving a lei (garland) made from flowers, leaves, shells, seeds, nuts, or feathers is a demonstration of love or honor. You can order real flower leis with orchids being the most popular for luaus due to their longevity, or you can purchase artificial leis from party supply stores in your area. Items we see at luaus on Mainland USA that do not belong at authentic luaus since they belong to Caribbean culture rather than Polynesian culture include flamingos, limbo sticks, and steel pan drum music.

Lei Greeting

DRESS

As you send invitations to your luau, encourage guests to dress Hawaiian style to add to the ambiance and aloha. Think comfort and color. Women in Hawaii can be seen wearing muumuu dresses that are light and flowing in either maxi or knee-length or other styles of dresses and skirts in floral or Hawaiian prints. Men usually opt for the Aloha shirt in bold prints that evolved from the Palaka shirts worn by plantation and dock workers. Sandals and slippahs (flip flops)are the footwear of choice for both women and men as they allow for comfort in grass or sand and are easily removed. A word on costumes: Leave the dance costumes to actual Hawaiian and Polynesian dancers. It is impossible to get it right and be respectful if you are not a student of the dance since every costume piece has symbolism behind it and is chosen for a specific performances and specific purposes. It is okay to purchase and wear the souvenir style, party costumes such as raffia skirts and artificial flowers that are available in party supply stores. Dancers' costumes are made from different materials and processes, and whether pieces are real or artificial, they are authentic representations of traditional dress.

MUSIC

To add to the authenticity of your luau, add soothing, Hawaiian music played on ukulele or slack key guitar. Try streaming from a radio station in Hawaii or create your own playlist with songs that have become popular for luaus. A mix of songs recognized around the world and others more so known by islanders is included below.

Hukilau
Tiny Bubbles
Blue Hawaii
Over the Rainbow
My Little Grass Shack
Hawaiian War Chant
Island Style
Ka Uluwehi O Ke Kai
Hanalei Moon
Waikiki
Sophisticated Hula
Aloha Oe

ENTERTAINMENT

For the best and most authentic luau, hire professional Polynesian entertainers. Most Polynesian entertainment companies on the mainland have founders who trained and performed in luau shows in Hawaii. They model their shows like the shows in Hawaii, with performances including a mixture of Hawaiian hula, Tahitian dance, New Zealand Māori dance, and Samoan fire knife. They usually offer packages of 1 dancer or more to fit any budget, whether it is a small, private party or a large, corporate-sponsored event. Beware of general entertainment companies and dancers of other genres who claim they can provide hula dancers as they are not representing Hawaii accurately and are doing a disservice to the culture and their clients. Hawaiian hula and other Polynesian dances require years of training to learn the languages, dances, and meanings as the dances are quite literal representations of important genealogies and histories of Hawaiian and Polynesian peoples. Polynesian dancers are passionate about sharing their culture and aloha spirit with you.

Hawaiian Hula: Hula uses the hands and body to tell the genealogies and history of the Hawaiians through oli (chants) and mele (songs) with kahiko being the ancient style and 'auana being modern with stringed instruments as accompaniment.

Tahitian Dance: Polynesians arrived in Tahiti prior to Hawaii and gifted Hawaii with one of the sacred drums, and Tahitian dances include drum dances like 'ote'a and 'aparima which is closer to hula.

New Zealand Māori Dance: Aotearoa was the last of the Polynesian islands to be settled, and dances include the haka war dance, poi ball dance, and action songs telling of their warrior qualities.

Samoan Dance: Upbeat dances with body slapping and fire knife demonstrating bravery are characteristic of Samoa.

Polynesian Instruments: Each Polynesian culture has unique drums and drumming style whether using gourd drums, slit log drums, or other percussion instruments, and the instrument most associated with Hawaii is the ukulele, a small, guitar-like instrument.

Hula Dancer

Tahitian Dancers

HAWAIIAN WORDS

Use signage such as banners with "Aloha" to greet your guests or as photography backdrops. Also try sprinkling some of the following Hawaiian words in conversation. You will also be prepared for your next trip to Hawaii.

Aloha: hello, goodbye, love
Mahalo: thank you
Ohana: family
`Aina: land
Hana Hou: one more time
A Hui Hou: until we meet again

MEANING OF ALOHA

Aloha is more than just a word or greeting. It is an attitude and way of life in Hawaii. Pilahi Paki was asked to speak to Hawaiian legislators about the meaning of aloha, and below are the words she spoke.

The "A" in aloha stands for "Akahi," meaning kindness, to be expressed with a feeling of tenderness.

The "L" in aloha stands for "Lokahi," meaning unity, to be expressed with a feeling of harmony.

The "O" in aloha stands for "`Olu`olu," meaning agreeable, to be expressed with a feeling of pleasantness.

The "H" in aloha stands for "Ha`aha`a," meaning humility, to be expressed with a feeling of modesty.

The final "A" in aloha stands for "Ahonui," meaning patience, to be expressed with a feeling of perseverance.

Waikiki Sunset

ABOUT THE AUTHOR

Dawn Mahealani Douglas is an award-winning entertainer, business owner, and activist. Named Best Entertainer Atlanta, she has performed 300 shows a year across 11 states and 3 countries. The founder of Mahealani's Polynesian Entertainment, an award-winning entertainment company named Best Event Entertainment Services Georgia, she also has a heart for serving God, women, and the planet and regularly volunteers her time for those causes. She is a halau trained, hula dancer and luau entertainer form the island of Oahu.

Made in the USA
Middletown, DE
02 April 2025